DO PENGUINS GET FROSTBITE?

Questions and Answers About Polar Animals

BY MELVIN AND GILDA BERGER
ILLUSTRATED BY HIGGINS BOND

SCHOLASTIC REFERENCE

CONTENTS

KEY TO ABBREVIATIONS
cm = centimeter/centimetre
kg = kilogram
km = kilometer/kilometre
km² = square kilometer/kilometre
kph = kilometers/kilometres per hour
m = meter/metre
°C = degrees Celsius
t = tonnes

Text copyright © 2000 by Melvin and Gilda Berger
Illustrations copyright © 2000 by Barbara Higgins Bond
All rights reserved. Published by Scholastic Inc.
SCHOLASTIC and associated logos are trademarks and/or registered trademarks of Scholastic Inc.

No part of this publication may be reproduced, or stored in a retrieval system, or transmitted in
any form or by any means, electronic, mechanical, photocopying, recording, or otherwise, without written permission of the publisher. For information regarding permission, write to
Scholastic Inc., Attention: Permissions Department, 555 Broadway, New York, NY 10012.

Library of Congress Cataloging-in-Publication Data

Berger, Melvin.
    Do penguins get frostbite?: questions and answers about polar animals / by Melvin and
    Gilda Berger; illustrated by Higgins Bond.
        p.   cm. — (Scholastic question and answer series)
    Includes index.
    Summary: Questions and answers present the habitats and behavior of a variety of polar
    animals, from penguins and arctic foxes to reindeer and baleen whales.
        1. Zoology—Polar regions—Miscellanea—Juvenile literature. [1. Zoology—Polar regions—
    Miscellanea. 2. Questions and answers.] I. Berger, Gilda. II. Bond, Higgins. III. Title.
QL104 .B474 2000   590'.911–dc21   00-025257

ISBN 0-439-19377-X

Book design by David Saylor and Nancy Sabato

10 9 8 7 6 5 4 3 2   01 02 03 04

Printed in Mexico.   08
First trade printing, November 2001

Expert Reader: Anthony Brownie, Supervisor, Animal Department
Central Park Wildlife Center, New York, NY

The penguins on the cover are emperor penguins. The seals on the title page are harp seals.

For Jacob, with love
— M. AND G. BERGER

This book is dedicated to my father, Henry Higgins Sr.,
who taught me to love and respect animals
— HIGGINS BOND

INTRODUCTION

You've probably seen polar animals in zoos—far from their homes around the North and South poles. But did you know that polar bears, reindeer, musk oxen, and arctic foxes come *only* from the Arctic, the region around the North Pole? And did you know that penguins and southern elephant seals come *only* from the Antarctic, the region around the South Pole?

Both polar regions are icy cold most of the year. But the Arctic is not quite as cold as the Antarctic. More land animals live in the Arctic because in summer the snow melts and the animals can feed on growing plants.

The Antarctic stays very cold—even in summer. The temperatures seldom rise above freezing. Most of the animals that live here are found in the sea.

Polar animals survive because they are specially fit for life in cold conditions. Land creatures have heavy coats to keep them warm. Many animals that live in the water have a thick layer of fat under their skin. Arctic foxes and deer are much smaller than their relatives in warmer climates. Smaller animals lose less body heat in freezing weather.

The regions around the North and South poles are cold and harsh. Yet some remarkable animals make their homes here. Life in the Arctic and the Antarctic is as rich and exciting as anywhere on Earth!

Melvin Berger   Gilda Berger

PENGUINS AND OTHER BIRDS

Do penguins get frostbite?

No. Penguins have a thick, waterproof covering of outer feathers and an inner layer of soft, fluffy feathers. The two layers of feathers form a kind of blanket to keep out the cold and hold in the body's heat. They protect the penguin's body parts from freezing or getting frostbite.

Where do penguins live?

In Antarctica, as well as in coastal areas touched by cold-water currents from Antarctica. Antarctica is the continent around the South Pole. It is larger than either Europe or Australia. All year long, the land is buried beneath a 1-mile-deep (1.6 km) layer of ice and snow.

How cold does it get in Antarctica?

Very cold. Winter in the Southern Hemisphere lasts from May through August. The surface of the water around Antarctica freezes into a solid sheet of ice. Frigid winds, with gusts as high as 120 miles an hour (190 kph), make the air feel much colder. The record for the lowest temperature on Earth, −128.6 degrees Fahrenheit (−89.1°C), was set in Antarctica on July 21, 1983.

Summer in the Southern Hemisphere, which lasts from December through February, is just slightly warmer. That's when chunks of ice break off and form immense icebergs. Some are as large as 5,000 square miles (13,000 km²)—the size of the state of Connecticut!

Where do penguins spend most of their time?

In the water. Penguins are birds that cannot fly. But they are excellent swimmers. Their small, strong wings serve as flippers, helping them paddle quickly through the water. The fastest swimmer, the gentoo penguin, has a maximum speed of about 17 miles an hour (27 kph)!

How long can penguins stay underwater?

No more than six minutes. After that, penguins need to breathe. They shoot out of the water, take a huge breath, and plunge back into the icy polar sea! This is called porpoising.

What do penguins eat?

Mostly fish, squid, and a kind of tiny animal called krill.

Which are the biggest penguins?

Emperor penguins. These large birds weigh about 100 pounds (45 kg) and are about 4 feet (1.2 m) tall—the height of an average second grader. The 15 other kinds of penguins vary in size. The smallest, called a rockhopper, is only about 1 foot (30 cm) tall.

An emperor penguin is credited with the deepest dive on record. In 1990, one went down about $1/3$ mile (0.5 km) in the Ross Sea, Antarctica.

How do penguins walk on ice?

With difficulty. Penguins look slow and clumsy as they strut across the ice on their two short legs. Their bodies sway from side to side while they hold their tiny wings straight out for balance.

But sometimes penguins are in a hurry. Then, they know how to put on speed. They get down on their bellies and push off with their feet and wings. Zoom! Away they go, sliding across the slippery ice.

Emperor penguins

Where do penguins lay their eggs?

On land. When ready, the pregnant female penguins jump up out of the water and onto the ice. Some waddle across the icy land for as far as 100 miles (160 km) to reach a safe nesting place, called a rookery. As many as one million birds nest in a rookery!

How do penguins make nests?

Unlike other birds. Penguins cannot make nests of grass or weeds since few plants grow in the Antarctic. Some penguins just lay their eggs on bare ground or ice. Others scrape a shallow hole in the ground that they line with pebbles.

How many eggs does the emperor penguin lay at a time?

Usually just one. As soon as the female lays the egg, she rolls it onto the feet of the male penguin. Then she hurries back to the water. The male covers the egg with a flap of his belly skin for warmth and waddles over to join a circle of other males.

For two months the male penguins stay huddled together in the circle without eating. Each one loses about half its weight. The penguins on the outside of the circle slowly work their way inside to warm up, while those on the inside move out to take their turn in the cold air. That's only fair!

How long does it take the eggs to hatch?

About 35 days. The young penguin is called a chick. For a short while, the male feeds the chick a milky substance from his mouth. Then the female returns to care for the chick. The male heads for the ocean waters to fill his empty stomach with food. When the male comes back a few weeks later, both parents look after the chick. They place partly digested food in its mouth and the chick grows quickly. In about six months the penguin chick is big enough to take care of itself.

Emperor penguins and chicks

Skua

Penguins

Which polar birds steal penguin eggs?

Skuas (SKOO-uhs). Large and fierce, the skuas feed on penguin eggs or even on young chicks that they snatch from the penguins' rookeries.

Skuas sometimes work in pairs to nab their prey. One skua sweeps down and uses its strong, hooked beak as a battering ram to knock over an adult penguin. The other skua, following close behind, drops from the sky and grabs a chick or an egg.

Skuas also steal prey over water. Working alone, a skua sights a bird carrying a fish. The skua slams into the bird, knocking the fish out of its mouth. Before you could even say, "Whoa!" the skua seizes the falling fish in midair and eats it.

Are skuas found only in Antarctica?

No. Some skuas also live in the Arctic. In fact, they're the only seabird that can be found in both the Antarctic *and* the Arctic.

Albatross

Petrel

Which is the largest polar bird?

The wandering albatross. In September 1965, sailors caught a male albatross with a wingspan of 11 feet, 11 inches (3.6 m). That's nearly twice as long as your bed!

Ocean voyagers tell us that albatrosses can glide on the wind for hours without once flapping their wings. Sometimes the birds follow a ship day after day, hardly ever touching down to rest. The only time they land is to breed and lay their eggs.

Which polar birds seem to walk on water?

Petrels. Most fly just above the ocean's surface. They let their legs hang down with sharp claws extended, ready to grab any fish they see below. From far away, it looks like the birds are walking on water.

Cousins of the albatross, petrels also stay mostly at sea. They fly over land only during the breeding season, or when a big storm at sea blows them ashore.

Willow ptarmigans in summer

Willow ptarmigans in winter

Which polar birds travel farther than any other bird?

Arctic terns. When it's summer in the Arctic, these seabirds breed and hatch their young. The terns stay there until it starts to grow colder. Then the adults and their young begin the long flight to Antarctica, where summer is beginning. The birds take about three months to make the 12,000-mile (19,300 km) trip.

The terns spend the three months of the Antarctic summer near the South Pole before flying north once more—another 12,000 miles (19,300 km). They arrive back in the Arctic around mid-June. What a life—two summers and no winters every single year!

Which Arctic bird changes color twice a year?

The willow ptarmigan (TAHR-mih-gun). Its feathers are white in winter. That's when the dry, treeless land around the Arctic Ocean, called the tundra, is snow-covered and the ptarmigan can hide in snowbanks.

But in the summer, when the ice on the tundra melts and small plants poke out of the ground, the ptarmigan's feathers change to the color of the earth. Then, few enemies can spot the ptarmigan as it sits on its leafy ground nest among rocks and low-growing plants. Even its brown-speckled eggs are hard to see.

What makes the ptarmigan change colors?

The number of daylight hours. As the days grow shorter in the fall, the ptarmigan's feathers begin turning white. As the days grow longer in the spring, the feathers start getting dark.

In one experiment, scientists kept a ptarmigan in a room without windows. They left the lights on for shorter and shorter lengths of time. The bird's feathers turned white, even though it was still the middle of the summer! The scientists proved that length of day, not temperature, makes the ptarmigan change colors.

POLAR BEARS AND OTHER LAND ANIMALS

Where do polar bears live?

Only in the Arctic. Polar bears wander on the tundra along the northern coasts of Canada, Greenland, Russia, and Alaska, as well as on the islands and in the waters of the Arctic Ocean. Sometimes polar bears drift about on gigantic pieces of floating ice, called ice floes. But, look as you might, you'll never find a polar bear in or near Antarctica!

Do polar bears stay mostly in groups or alone?

Alone. But during the winter, polar bears live together in dens that the females dig in the snow. Pregnant bears give birth to their cubs in late November or early December.

What keeps polar bears warm?

Thick fur, a 4-inch (10 cm) layer of fat under their skin, and furry feet. The polar bear's dense fur is made up of hairs that are actually hollow, transparent tubes. Sunlight passes through the tubes, striking the polar bear's black skin and warming its body. Meanwhile, the air trapped inside the hollow hairs acts as insulation. It holds in the bear's body heat and keeps out the icy cold. Hairy soles keep its feet warm and help it walk on the ice without slipping.

How long do polar bears live?

Polar bears in the Arctic generally live up to 33 years.

Which is faster—a running bear or a swimming bear?

A running bear. On land, a polar bear can run up to 35 miles an hour (56 kph). A swimming bear, paddling its fastest, clocks only about 6 miles an hour (10 kph).

Yet, compared to humans, polar bears are champion athletes. They can move on land and in water three times faster than the swiftest Olympic long-distance runners and swimmers!

Arctic

North America

How many bear cubs are born at once?

Usually only one cub is born at a time. Despite the huge size of an adult polar bear, the newborn cub is just 9 inches (22.9 cm) long and has a birth weight of about 1¹/₂ pounds (0.68 kg).

Here's a surprising fact: Polar bear babies are small enough to stay safe and warm between the toes of their mother's front paws!

Are female polar bears good mothers?

Yes—the best. In the den, the mothers carefully guard their cubs for the first three months. Day by day, the cubs grow bigger and stronger, feeding on the mother bears' milk.

When the young are ready to leave the den, their mothers teach them how to hunt for seals, walruses, and fish. If meat is scarce, the mother bears show the cubs how to search for berries and other plants they can eat.

After two years, the "babies" are about 10 feet (3 m) long and tip the scales at nearly 1,500 pounds (680 kg)! Now they're fully grown and ready to care for themselves.

Polar bear cub

Polar bears

What is a polar bear's main food?

Seals—especially the kind called ringed seals. Polar bears usually wait, silent and unmoving, for up to four hours near holes in the ice where the seals come up to breathe.

As soon as a seal rises to the surface, WHAM! The polar bear slams it with a single killing blow of its powerful paw. Then, using its paws and teeth, the bear hauls the seal out of the water and swallows its fill of sealskin, fat, and organs. After one such meal, a polar bear can go up to five days without eating again.

Polar bear

Do polar bears always kill seals with the same paw?

It seems so. Observers report that polar bears always attack seals with their left paw. Perhaps they're naturally lefty.

When do polar bears launch surprise attacks?

Usually in the spring, when the Arctic ice is breaking up. Instead of waiting on top of the ice, the polar bear swims toward an ice floe where seals are resting.

When the polar bear gets close, it dives under the ice floe. Then it rears up, ramming the ice so hard that the seals topple into the water. The rest is easy. The bear grabs a seal, hauls it to land or onto an ice floe, and enjoys its meal.

What is the polar bear's sharpest sense?

Smell. Polar bears can detect the odor of a seal from as far away as 20 miles (32 km). They can even sniff out seal dens that are buried under layers of snow and ice. Experts say that a polar bear's sense of smell is about 100 times better than that of a human!

Do polar bears kill people?

Very rarely. Polar bears sometimes stalk humans as though they were prey. But the bears almost never kill people. Even hunters who shoot or trap bears for their fur are not attacked by these creatures. Experts say this may be the reason polar bears are endangered animals. There are only about 25,000 polar bears left in the entire world.

Why do arctic foxes follow polar bears?

To eat the bears' leftovers. But the foxes have to be careful. If they get too close, they may become meals for the polar bears!

How big are arctic foxes?

Not big at all. A full-grown arctic fox is only about the size of a very large house cat.

The arctic fox's small body surface loses less heat to the cold air than the body of a larger animal would. Also, short ears and a small snout help the arctic fox conserve heat in the severe polar cold.

What color are arctic foxes?

Brownish gray in summer; white in winter. The seasonal change in fur color allows arctic foxes to sneak up on their prey more easily. The dark summer color makes them hard to spot against the dirt that pokes through the melting snow. White is their camouflage in the snow.

Do arctic foxes hunt for food?

Yes. Arctic foxes prey on smaller animals, such as hares, squirrels, and birds. A particular favorite of foxes is small, long-haired, mouselike creatures called lemmings. Lemmings are the most common animal found in the far north.

How do arctic foxes catch lemmings?

They sniff them out. The arctic fox trots along, snout to the ground, picking up scents. Sooner or later, it picks up the smell of lemmings hidden in a burrow. The fox stops and rears up on its back paws. Then, with full force, it crashes down on the burrow, front paws first. The lemmings don't have the chance to escape. One hungry arctic fox can devour 10 plump lemmings in a single day!

Arctic foxes in summer

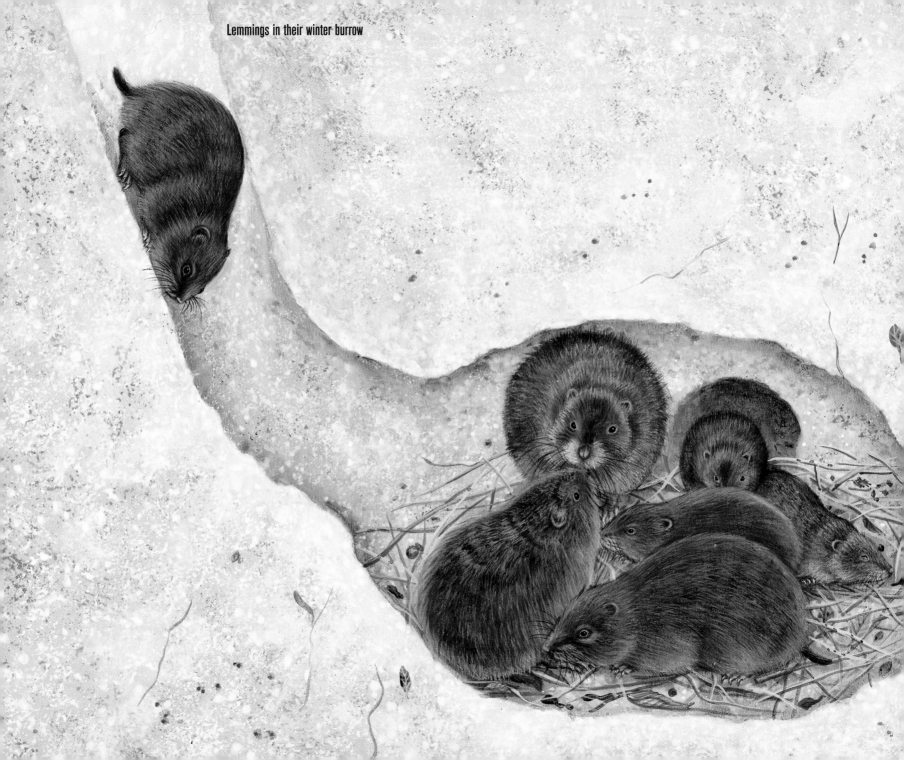

Lemmings in their winter burrow

Do lemmings eat smaller animals?

No. Lemmings are plant eaters. They feed on grasses and other small tundra plants that poke into their burrows. In turn, lemmings are eaten by foxes and other hungry predators, such as snowy owls and stoats. A stoat in its white winter coat is called an ermine.

How many offspring do female lemmings bear?

As many as 10 young at a time. And a female lemming can have three litters a year!

To add to the numbers, baby lemmings are ready to give birth to offspring themselves when they're only one month old. Lemmings multiply so fast that a colony is soon jam-packed with millions of creatures.

What happens when the colony gets overcrowded?

There's not enough food for everyone. Some lemmings flee the colony. Others follow. Soon, millions of lemmings are madly dashing away.

Foxes or owls use this opportunity to grab and eat these little animals. Some lemmings fall off cliffs. A good number accidentally drown while swimming.

The lemmings that were left behind now have plenty of food and room. They breed and multiply. Eventually, the colony gets overcrowded and the pattern repeats itself.

Do fleeing lemmings kill themselves?

No. One of the most common myths about lemmings is that they drown themselves on purpose, not by accident. Scientists no longer believe this to be true. And neither should you!

Are wolverines small wolves?

No. Wolverines are related to weasels, not wolves. Wolverines live in the tundra around the Arctic Circle.

What is the wolverine's greatest enemy?

Humans. Hunters trap and kill wolverines for their fur. Their coats, ranging in color from dark brown to black with a band of lighter-colored hair along the sides, make wolverine fur attractive and valuable. Farmers and ranchers also hunt wolverines because they sometimes kill poultry and livestock. As a result, there are few wolverines left in the wild.

What do wolverines eat?

Almost anything. Their summer diet includes small mammals, birds, and plants. But in winter they prefer big game, such as reindeer.

A wolverine hunts a reindeer by jumping on its back from a tree or a rock. With its powerful claws and sharp teeth, the wolverine digs into the reindeer's flesh and holds on until the reindeer collapses and falls to the ground. Then it tears apart the body, eating some chunks right away and hiding the rest to eat later. Although a reindeer is five times the size of a wolverine, it almost always falls victim to the smaller animal. Reindeer seem to have no way of warding off the attack of a hungry wolverine.

Are reindeer the same as other deer?

No. Reindeer have larger antlers than the males of most other kinds of deer. Also, reindeer are the only deer in which both males and females have antlers.

Wider hoofs also fit reindeer for life in the polar regions. Their big feet save them from sinking into deep snow during the winter and into mud when the snow on the tundra melts in summer.

Wolverine

Reindeer

Reindeer

How do male reindeer use their antlers?

As weapons. Male reindeer, called bulls, fight other males to determine which deer will lead the herd. The winning male also attracts female reindeer, called cows, with which he mates. In the spring, the cows usually give birth to offspring, called calves.

Some reindeer battles can be deadly. When two reindeer charge each other, their antlers may lock together. If neither one can break free, both animals starve to death because they can't hunt for food or eat.

How do female reindeer use their antlers?

No one is sure. Some scientists think the females use their antlers to scrape away snow to reach buried plants. Females may also fight one another when food is scarce.

Where do reindeer find food?

It depends on the weather. When snow covers the tundra, the reindeer sniff around for traces of low-growing plants, such as moss and lichen (LYE-kun). With their snouts or hoofs, they scrape away the snow to get to the plants. A reindeer needs to eat about 26 pounds (11.8 kg) of food every day to survive.

In the winter months, when the ground freezes over, giant herds of reindeer migrate, or move, to find plants to eat. They may travel hundreds of miles (kilometers), swimming across streams or rivers in their path, to reach forests at the southern edge of the Arctic region.

In the forests, the reindeer eat steadily until summer. Then they gather in herds and tramp back toward the North Pole, arriving in time to feed on the new plant growth. Here they stay until the ground freezes over.

Which animals stay on the tundra all winter?

Musk oxen. These big, gentle creatures wander the Arctic tundra in summer and winter, grazing on grasses, willow and pine shoots, lichen, and moss. When food grows scarce, the musk oxen depend mainly on lichen and on fat stored up in their bodies. After all, musk oxen have plenty of fat to spare. An adult male can weigh more than 900 pounds (408 kg).

How long is the fur of a musk ox?

The longest of any animal. The hairs of the musk ox's coat can be 3 feet (1 m) long!

Two layers of long, shaggy hair—a coarse coat on the outside and a fine, soft one underneath—keep the musk ox from feeling the frigid Arctic cold.

Its insulation is so good, in fact, that a musk ox can lie down on the snow without freezing—and without melting the snow under its body!

What do musk oxen do when under attack?

They form a circle, shoulder to shoulder facing out, with young members of the herd in the middle. Few enemies can get past the musk oxens' sharp, 2-foot-long (61 cm) horns.

Nevertheless, once in a while a hungry wolf tries to force its way into the circle. Then, one of the musk oxen lowers its horns and charges. The musk ox may slam straight into the wolf, breaking its bones. Or it may stab the animal with its horns. Experts say that a charging musk ox has the force of a truck traveling 17 miles an hour (27 kph)!

What is the musk ox's most dangerous foe?

A mosquito! This tiny insect may carry the germs for several diseases that can kill a musk ox. Since it's hard for the mosquito to bite through the long hair, a determined mosquito just nips the musk ox on its snout!

Musk oxen

Arctic hares

Where did the snowshoe hare get its name?

From its big, broad hind feet. The feet, which look and work like snowshoes, let the hare run, walk, and jump on soft snow without sinking in. Meanwhile, long hairs between the toes and on the soles keep the hare's feet from freezing and slipping on the slick snow or ice. Like other Arctic animals, the snowshoe hare is well camouflaged. Its fur is white in winter and brown in summer.

Are hares different from rabbits?

Yes. You can tell the difference most easily in newborn animals. Hares are born with fur and with their eyes open. Rabbits, on the other hand, have no fur at birth and their eyes are still closed. Also, rabbits escape from their enemies by hiding. Hares escape by running away quickly in a kind of gallop.

   Adult hares usually have longer ears than full-grown rabbits. But arctic hares are the exception. They have short ears—probably to conserve body heat. Arctic hares also have shorter snouts than rabbits—another way of staying warm.

How do arctic hares escape their enemies?

They flee. Sometimes a fox or a wolf comes upon a group of arctic hares on the tundra. As soon as they see the enemy, the hares scatter. By running off in all directions, they confuse the attacker and make their escape. The frightened hares look like snowballs bouncing across the tundra!

What are baby arctic hares called?

Leverets. The female arctic hare gives birth to her leverets on the ground or in a hollow that she scratches out in the dirt. One litter contains four to eight leverets. They are usually born in June. Their fur is darker than that of adult hares.

WHALES AND OTHER SEA CREATURES

Are whales polar animals?

Some are. In summer, these whales swim to the icy waters of the Arctic or the Antarctic. They feed on the tiny animals called krill that live there. When winter comes, the whales move to warmer, calmer seas to mate and bear their young. But the whales don't eat here. Instead, they live off the fat that they built up in the polar oceans.

With the return of warm weather in the late spring, the whales journey back to the polar feeding areas. Many whales migrate thousands of miles (kilometers) between polar seas and warmer waters every year.

What keeps whales warm in icy water?

Thick skin and blubber. The sperm whale has some of the best protection. Its skin is 14 inches (35.6 cm) thick. And the blubber, a layer of fat below the skin, extends down another 2 feet (61 cm). Even when it swims in icy water, the sperm whale's double wrapping keeps it warm and comfortable.

Can whales get too warm?

Yes, indeed. If whales swim very fast for a long time—even in polar waters—they may become overheated. But they have a special way to cool off.

Whales have large blood vessels that carry blood throughout their bodies. When a whale gets very warm, extra blood flows to its skin. The cold ocean water cools its blood, which cools down the whale. What great air conditioning!

Sperm whales

Bowhead whale

Krill

Baleen

Which kinds of whales migrate?

Baleen whales. Instead of teeth, each baleen whale has long, comblike plates, called baleen, hanging down from the roof of its mouth. The baleen is made of the same material as your fingernails. Some kinds of baleen whales swim north from warm waters to the Arctic; others swim south to the Antarctic.

How do baleen whales get their food?

They swim along with their mouths wide open. Thousands of gallons (liters) of water flow in. The water is full of krill that swarm by the millions in the upper layers of the polar oceans.

    With their giant tongues, the whales squeeze the water out through the baleen. The krill get trapped on the baleen plates and then, GULP, the whales swallow them all!

How much krill do baleen whales eat?

Tons. Blue whales, the largest of all whales, fill their stomachs with as much as 4 tons (4 t) of krill every single day!

Which baleen whale never leaves the Arctic?

The bowhead whale. This whale, also called the Greenland right whale, does not migrate. It spends the entire year in the Arctic Ocean.

    The bowhead whale has the longest baleen of any whale. Each plate can be 15 feet (4.6 m) long! If laid out on a basketball court, one plate would stretch from the foul line to the basket!

Do toothed whales migrate?

Most do not. Toothed whales, which are whales with teeth instead of baleen, usually stay in one place. Belugas and narwhals (NAR-wollz) are two kinds of toothed whales that swim in Arctic waters year-round. They are small whales that seldom grow more than 16 feet (5 m) long.

How can you tell belugas from narwhals?

Easily. The beluga is completely white, from snout to tail. In fact, people sometimes call the beluga the white whale. Also, a beluga's body is narrow at both ends.

You cannot miss a narwhal, with an extremely long tusk sticking out of its mouth. This sharp, twisted tusk is really one of the narwhal's two teeth. But no one is sure of its purpose. It may be a spear for catching fish, a tool for digging shellfish out of the ocean bottom, or a weapon that males use for fighting other males during the mating season. It certainly can't be used for chewing!

Belugas

Narwhals

Are orcas polar animals?

Yes and no. Large numbers of these toothed whales live year-round in the waters of the Antarctic. Others are found there only part of the year.

In the Antarctic, the orcas usually hunt in pods, or groups, of 5 to 20 whales. Their main prey are seals, penguins, and baleen whales. Orcas especially like the tongues and lips of baleen whales. They rip out bite-sized chunks and swallow them whole.

Because orcas attack and eat many animals that live in the sea, they are sometimes called killer whales. But, when captured, the orcas prove to be gentle creatures—easy to train and rarely vicious to humans.

Orca

Which toothed whales migrate every summer?

Male sperm whales—the largest of the toothed whales. Both male and female sperm whales spend the winter in warm waters. But when summer comes, some males migrate to the polar regions.

The sperm whale hunts giant squid in the cold water near both poles. To catch one of these creatures, the whales dive down as deep as $1\frac{1}{2}$ miles (2.4 km) and hold their breath for up to two hours.

Because giant squid seldom come to the surface, few people have ever seen one. Yet we know that they exist. Cuts and scars on the bodies of sperm whales tell the story of mighty battles between the whales and the squid.

How big are giant squid?

Very big. Giant squid can grow to be 60 feet (18 m) long. Lay one down on a baseball diamond and it will reach from the batter's box to the pitcher's mound. At 440 pounds (200 kg), a giant squid weighs as much as a full-sized gorilla.

The giant squid is related to the octopus. But instead of having eight arms like an octopus, the squid is equipped with ten arms. Each arm has rows of suckers to catch and hold the fish that squid prey on.

Are all squids giant-sized?

No, most are much smaller. Squids range in length between 1 foot (30 cm) and nearly 40 feet (12 m). They are among the most common animals in the ocean.

Squids are an important link in the chain of life in the ocean. The usual squid diet includes small fish, shellfish, and other sea creatures. Squids, in turn, are eaten by larger creatures, such as whales, large fish, seals, and seabirds.

How do squid move through water?

By jet action. A squid pulls water into its body through slits behind its head and then shoots the water out at high speed. This jet action moves the squid through the water very fast. Small wonder some people call these animals sea arrows!

What do squids do when attacked?

They squirt out an inky substance. The "ink" hides the squid and confuses its enemies while it swims speedily away. Fast swimming and a big supply of ink make the squid one terrific escape artist.

Sperm whale

Squid

Where do most seals live?

In the Arctic or northern seas. Among the most common is the ringed seal. Scientists guess about six million ringed seals live in the Arctic waters, feeding mainly on small shrimp and other shellfish. You can easily spot these seals by the ringlike markings on their fur.

The ringed seal is the smallest kind of seal. Each is only about 5 feet (1.5 m) long and weighs no more than 200 pounds (91 kg). When swimming, seals need to come up for air every few minutes. They must either find a breathing hole or make one by chewing through the ice. With no way to defend themselves, ringed seals make easy prey for polar bears, which often lie in wait for them at their breathing holes.

Which is the largest seal?

A kind of elephant seal found mostly in waters near Antarctica. The male grows to be about 21 feet (6.4 m) long and weighs up to 8,000 pounds (3,600 kg). The seal got its name from its long snout—which looks like an elephant's trunk—and its wrinkled skin.

An elephant seal has a thick coat of fur that it sheds every year. Unlike some other seals that lose a few hairs at a time, huge patches of fur fall off the elephant seal at one time. Its messy looks don't improve until the new fur grows in!

Do seals lay eggs?

No. Seals are mammals, just like humans are. The young develop inside the mother's body and are born alive.

In the spring, seals go to breeding grounds on land, called rookeries, to give birth. Some rookeries have thousands of seals. A female seal usually has one baby, called a pup, at a time. The pup grows fast on the rich milk it gets from its mother.

At birth, a northern fur seal, for example, weighs about 10 pounds (4.5 kg). But within three months, the pup triples its weight and can care for itself.

Elephant seals

Walruses

Which arctic seal has tusks?

The walrus. The tusks are really two upper teeth that stick out of the walrus's mouth. The tusks of females are thin, curved, and about 2 feet (61 cm) long. The tusks of males are straighter, thicker, and somewhat longer.

The male with the longest tusks usually becomes the leader of the group. If two males have tusks of about the same length, they may fight each other. Each one tries to stab the other with its tusks.

Sometimes walruses use their tusks as tools. By jabbing the points into the ice, the walruses can haul their bodies out of the water and onto land. Or, they put the two tusks to work cracking breathing holes in the ice.

What is a walrus's favorite food?

Clams. The stiff, sensitive whiskers on its snout probably help the walrus find its food in the dark sea waters. The walrus then shovels the clams into its mouth. With its tongue, the animal sucks out the flesh and spits out the shell.

A walrus can dive down 300 feet (91 m) to reach the clams and other shellfish that live on the muddy ocean bottom. It feeds steadily for as long as 25 minutes. Before it comes up for air, a walrus can gulp down as many as 4,000 clams!

Do walruses live alone or in groups?

In groups. Each group, or herd, may include more than 100 walruses. Walruses tend to haul themselves out of the water between feedings and huddle together on ice or land— sometimes one on top of another. This may help the walruses stay warm. It may also just make them feel good to be near one another.

Do people live in the Arctic?

Yes. The Arctic is home to many different peoples. For thousands of years, the Inuit have lived in Greenland, Alaska, Canada, and Siberia; the Nenet in north central Siberia; and the Lapps in northern Scandinavia. Among others closely tied to the Arctic land are the Aleuts, who live on islands near Alaska.

To survive, these people have fished and hunted polar animals for generations. They eat their meat and make clothes out of their hides. They even raise reindeer for milk, and to pull sleighs and carry loads.

But now other people are coming to the far north. Some of them are killing large numbers of animals just for their fur and skins. Many are digging wells to find oil and mining the land for coal and copper.

The new ways of life in the Arctic region are harming the polar animals. Polar bears, musk oxen, and some kinds of seals and whales were close to extinction until laws were passed to protect them.

Reindeer

45

A scientific research station in Antarctica

Emperor penguins

Do people live in Antarctica?

No. But scientists come to Antarctica for short periods of time. They explore the land and study the climate and atmosphere. They also gather information about the animals that make their homes at the bottom of the world.

Antarctica does not belong to any one nation. It is a special example of cooperation among different peoples. In 1959, 12 nations, including the United States, Australia, Great Britain, Chile, and Norway, signed a treaty agreeing to use Antarctica only for peaceful purposes, and to protect its environment.

Antarctica remains a barren continent where the ice almost never melts. Penguins live there on land year-round, and the seas are always full of fish and other sea life. In the summer, seals and seabirds come to join them, along with migrating whales. Let's hope it always stays that way!

INDEX

About the Authors

Someday the Bergers hope to see polar animals in their native homes. Until then, they are happy to visit polar bears, penguins, seals, and other animals from the North and South poles at New York City's outstanding Central Park Zoo.

About the Illustrator

Higgins Bond especially loves to illustrate books about animals and nature. She lives in Nashville, Tennessee, with her son and an animal that loves cold weather—a Siberian husky named Simba.